Addiction

Distinguishing Between Fact and Opinion

Curriculum Consultant: JoAnne Buggey, Ph.D.
College of Education, University of Minnesota

By Bradley Steffens

Greenhaven Press, Inc.
Post Office Box 289009
San Diego, CA 92198-9009

Titles in the opposing viewpoints juniors series:

Acid Rain	Endangered Species	Police Brutality
Addiction	The Environment	Pollution
Advertising	Forests	Population
AIDS	Free Speech	Poverty
Alcohol	Garbage	Prisons
Animal Rights	Gun Control	Smoking
Causes of Crime	The Homeless	Television
Child Abuse	Hunger	Toxic Wastes
Christopher Columbus	Immigration	The U.S. Constitution
Death Penalty	Nuclear Power	The War on Drugs
Drugs and Sports	The Palestinian Conflict	Working Mothers
Elections	Patriotism	Zoos

Cover photo: COMSTOCK

Library of Congress Cataloging-in-Publication Data

Steffens, Bradley, 1956-
   Addiction : distinguishing between fact and opinion / by Bradley Steffens ; curriculum consultant, JoAnne Buggey.
     p. cm. — (Opposing viewpoints juniors)
   Includes bibliographical references and index.
   ISBN 1-56510-094-8 (alk. paper)
   1. Drug abuse—Juvenile literature. 2. Addicts—Juvenile literature. [1. Drug abuse. 2. Critical thinking.] I. Buggey, JoAnne. II. Title. III. Series.
HV5801.S764 1994
362.29—dc20   93-29058
                                                                                CIP
                                                                                AC

No part of this book may be reproduced or used in any other form or by any other means, electrical, mechanical, or otherwise, including, but not limited to, photocopy, recording, or any information storage and retrieval system, without prior written permission from the publisher.

Copyright 1994 by Greenhaven Press, Inc.
Printed in the U.S.A.

CONTENTS

The Purpose of This Book:	An Introduction to Opposing Viewpoints	4
Skill Introduction:	What Is the Difference Between Fact and Opinion?	5
Sample Viewpoint A:	I think people who take drugs are sick	6
Sample Viewpoint B:	I think people who take drugs are stupid	7
Analyzing the Sample Viewpoints:	Tallying the Facts and Opinions	8

Chapter 1
Preface: Is Addiction a Serious Problem? 9
Viewpoint 1: Addiction is a serious problem 10
Viewpoint 2: Addiction is exaggerated 12
Critical Thinking Skill 1: Tallying the Facts and Opinions 14

Chapter 2
Preface: Should Addiction Be Treated as a Disease? 15
Viewpoint 3: Addiction should be treated as a disease 16
Viewpoint 4: Addiction should not be treated as a disease 18
Critical Thinking Skill 2: Distinguishing Between Fact and Opinion 20

Chapter 3
Preface: Should Drugs Be Legalized? 21
Viewpoint 5: Legalizing drugs would reduce addiction 22
Viewpoint 6: Legalizing drugs would increase addiction 24
Critical Thinking Skill 3: Understanding Editorial Cartoons 26

Chapter 4
Preface: What Should the Government Do to Reduce Addiction? 27
Viewpoint 7: The government should spend more on drug law enforcement 28
Viewpoint 8: The government should spend more on drug treatment 30
Critical Thinking Skill 4: Using Facts and Opinions 32

For Further Reading 33
Works Consulted 33
Organizations to Contact 35
Index 36

THE PURPOSE OF THIS BOOK

An Introduction to Opposing Viewpoints

When people disagree, it is hard to figure out who is right. You may decide one person is right just because the person is your friend or relative. But this is not a very good reason to agree or disagree with someone. It is better if you try to understand why these people disagree. On what main points do they differ? Read or listen to each person's argument carefully. Separate the facts and opinions that each person presents. Finally, decide which argument best matches what you think. This process, examining an argument without emotion, is part of what critical thinking is all about.

This is not easy. Many things make it hard to understand and form opinions. People's values, ages, and experiences all influence the way they think. This is why learning to read and think critically is an invaluable skill.

Opposing Viewpoints Juniors books will help you learn and practice skills to improve your ability to read critically. By reading opposing views on an issue, you will become familiar with methods people use to attempt to convince you that their point of view is right. And you will learn to separate the authors' opinions from the facts they present.

Each Opposing Viewpoints Juniors book focuses on one critical thinking skill that will help you judge the views presented. Some of these skills are telling the difference between fact and opinion, recognizing propaganda techniques, and locating and analyzing the main idea. These skills will allow you to examine opposing viewpoints more easily. The viewpoints are placed in a running debate and are always placed with the pro view first.

SKILL INTRODUCTION

What Is the Difference Between Fact and Opinion?

In this Opposing Viewpoints Juniors book you will be asked to identify and study statements of fact and statements of opinion. A fact is a statement that can be proved true. Here are some examples of factual statements: "In 1970 the United States Congress voted to ban all cigarette advertising from television," "The average American television viewer sees over one hundred commercials a day," and "Over 100,000 Americans die each year from alcohol-related deaths." It is fairly easy to prove these facts true. For instance, a historian one hundred years from now might need to prove that cigarette ads were banned from television and radio. One way she might do this is to check congressional records in Washington, D.C. There she could find a source to verify the year the ban took effect. Other facts may not be as easy to prove. And some ideas that are stated as fact may not be. In this book you will be asked to question facts presented in the viewpoints and be given some ways in which you might go about proving them.

Statements of opinion cannot be proved. An opinion is a statement that expresses how a person feels about something or what a person thinks is true. Remember the facts we mentioned? They can be easily changed into statements of opinion. For example, "The ban on cigarette advertising has not improved Americans' health," "Today's commercials are better than ever," and "Alcohol ads are responsible for the nation's high alcoholism rate," are all statements of opinion. They express what one person believes to be true. Opinions are not better than facts. They are different. Opinions are based on many things, including religious, social, moral, and family values. Opinions can also be based on medical and scientific facts. For instance, many scientists have made intelligent guesses about other planets based on what they know is true about earth. The only way these scientists would know their opinions were right is if they were able to visit other planets and test their guesses. Until their guesses are proved, then, they remain opinions. Some people have opinions that we do not like, or with which we disagree. That does not always make their opinions wrong—or right. There is room in our world for many different opinions.

When you read differing views on any issue, it is very important to know when people are using facts and when they are using opinions in an argument. When writers use facts, their arguments are often more believable and easier to prove. The more facts the author has, the more the reader can tell that the writer's opinion is based on something other than personal feelings.

Viewpoints of authors that base their arguments mostly on their own opinions, then, are impossible to prove factually true. This does not mean that these types of arguments are not meaningful. It means that you, as the reader, must decide whether you agree or disagree based on personal reasons, not factual ones.

We asked two students to give their opinions about drug addicts. Examine their viewpoints. Look for facts and opinions in their arguments.

SAMPLE VIEWPOINT A *Jan:*

I think people who take drugs are sick.

People who are addicted to drugs do not take them for fun. They take them because they are sick. These people cannot help themselves. They have a disease, and this disease is more powerful than their willpower. Some people think drug addicts can just stop taking drugs if they really want to, but this is not true. They need medical help. Doctors understand this about drug addiction. That is why the American Medical Association calls drug addiction a disease and thousands of hospitals have drug treatment centers. We should stop treating drug addicts like scum. They have a problem. We should offer them help.

SAMPLE VIEWPOINT B *Ron:*

> I think people who take drugs are stupid.

Drug addicts are the most selfish people in the world. They are willing to do anything to get high. They lie, they cheat, they steal. Most of the people in prison committed crimes involving drugs or while high on drugs. Drug addicts hurt their families, their friends, their employers, and even themselves, just to get a certain feeling from a drug. That is stupid. What is even more stupid is to feel sorry for them. Any addict can kick the drug habit if he or she really wants to. The only time treatment programs work is when the addict has decided to quit using drugs. Instead of babying drug addicts, society should punish them. That way, they will decide to quit using drugs sooner or decide never to start in the first place.

ANALYZING THE SAMPLE VIEWPOINTS

Jan and Ron have very different opinions about addicts. Both use facts and opinions in their arguments.

Jan:

FACTS

The American Medical Association calls drug addiction a disease.

Thousands of hospitals have drug treatment centers.

OPINIONS

We should stop treating drug addicts like scum.

We should offer drug addicts help.

Ron:

FACTS

Most of the people in prison committed crimes involving drugs or while high on drugs.

The only time treatment programs work is when the addict has decided to quit using drugs.

OPINIONS

Drug addicts are the most selfish people in the world.

Society should punish drug addicts.

In this sample, Jan and Ron have an equal number of facts and opinions. Which viewpoint did you find most convincing? Think of a fact and an opinion you have about addiction. As you read the viewpoints in this book, keep a tally like the one above to compare the author's arguments.

CHAPTER 1

PREFACE: Is Addiction a Serious Problem?

According to the Federal Bureau of Investigation (FBI), 28 million Americans used an illegal drug in 1988. Many people find the widespread use of illegal drugs to be alarming. They point to the damage caused by drug use—for example, emotional pain, increased crime, and lost productivity on the job—and say that drug addiction is the major problem facing the nation today.

Other people are not alarmed. They argue that drug use seems to be on the decline. According to the National Institute on Drug Abuse, the number of users of illegal drugs fell from 23 million in 1985 to 14.5 million in 1991. Besides, these people maintain, many people who are classified as regular drug users pose no real risk to themselves or society.

The first two viewpoints in this book debate the question of whether or not drug addiction is a serious problem. As you read these viewpoints, look for the facts and opinions the author presents. Which case is more strongly based on fact?

VIEWPOINT 1 Addiction is a serious problem

> **Editor's Note:** The author argues that the problem of drug addiction has become a worldwide crisis. Remember to keep a tally of the facts and opinions the author uses to persuade you to agree with him.

Dr. Coleman's statement about drug addiction is an opinion.

William F. Alden's estimates of drug users are based on government statistics, so they are facts.

In his book *Addicts and Addiction*, Dr. Vernon Coleman, a distinguished British doctor and author, calls drug addiction "the 20th Century plague." This is not an exaggeration. Like the plagues of old, drug addiction is killing millions of people worldwide and hurting the economies of many nations. The harm of addiction is not limited to the addicts themselves. Coleman estimates that for each addict there are at least five other people whose lives are hurt by the addiction. Drug addiction is a crisis of major proportions.

The problem is especially bad in the United States. One out of every ten Americans uses drugs, according to William F. Alden, the chief of the Office of Congressional and Public Affairs in the Drug

Washington, D.C., as an Example of the Far-Reaching Cost of Drug Abuse

Public Housing
Public housing costs to replace light bulbs shot out by drug dealers doubled from a 1985 pre-crack epidemic rate of **$3,600** to **$7,200** per complex in 1990.

Officials at the **Montana Terrace housing project** built a **$65,000** wrought iron fence to keep drug dealers from going through the 7-acre complex. Drug dealers immediately removed a 5-foot section of the fence with a blow torch.

Typical cost to clean and paint vacated public housing unit is **$1,000**. When vacated after use as a crack house, however, turnover costs can be as high as **$10,000**.

The drug business proliferates in inner-city housing projects.

Law Enforcement
Total police budget rose from pre-crack level of **$143.5 million** in 1985 to **$257 million** in 1991. Full-time police positions rose from **4,534** to **6,102** in the same period. Police say all increases can be attributed to drugs and related violence.

Operation Clean Sweep, an intensive 18-month police assault on open-air drug markets, cost **$20 million** to **$30 million** in the late '80s.

DRUG DEALERS
Turf battles among drug dealers accounted for a large share of the city's **483 murders** in 1990.

Drug offenders filter through justice system.

Courts
Costs for the **Counsel for Child Abuse and Neglect**—a program run by attorneys to represent children—increased 55 percent between 1989 and 1990, from **$1,077,092** to **$1,677,488**.

8 new judges added to Washington courts by Congress added annual costs of **$1.3 million**.

Neglect cases prosecuted by the city Department of Human Services increased from **496** in 1985 to **1,024** in 1989.

Siblings often raise siblings when a drug-addicted mother leaves home.

DRUG USERS
1 in 40 people in Washington is classified as a hard-core cocaine addict.

New transitional treatment program with 256 beds for prisoner addicts will cost about **$55 per day** or **$20,000 per year** for each person. 80% of the correction system's 9,000 inmates have had drug abuse problems.

A boarder baby abandoned at birth can cost a hospital **$200,000 a year** for legal, social, and pediatric services. The typical stay is 3 to 4 months. There were over 200 boarder babies in 1990.

In D.C. 1 in 10 babies is born to a drug-addicted mother.

Corrections
In 1990, **drug offenses** accounted for 44.8 percent of incarcerations, or 3,790 prisoners. The average daily cost per prisoner in 1990 was **$50 a day**, or **$18,000 a year**.

Medical Costs
D.C. hospitals had **$200 million** in unreimbursed expenses in 1990, much of it due to drug-related problems.

The District of Columbia typically pays **$20,000 to $30,000** for the first six weeks of care for a sick or premature drug-exposed baby. It can cost **$3,000 a day** to keep a baby in an intensive care unit. It is believed that 20 to 40 percent of babies born in the district have been exposed to illicit drugs.

There are **600 inpatient drug treatment beds** in the District of Columbia and **4,000 outpatient** slots, with a constant waiting list. A 28-day inpatient bed costs up to **$11,200**, at **$250 to $400** a day.

60 percent of new AIDS cases in the district were intravenous drug users.

Source: *The Christian Science Monitor*

Enforcement Administration. Alden claims that between 3 and 7 percent of Americans use an illegal drug on a daily basis. These figures do not include the use or abuse of alcohol, which is the number one drug used in the United States. The National Institute on Alcohol Abuse states that there are nearly 18 million alcoholics and alcohol abusers in the United States—about 7 percent of the population.

> The National Institute on Alcohol Abuse keeps statistics on alcohol abuse, so these figures can be considered facts.

These are frightening statistics, but the scariest thing about the plague of drugs is that it is spreading rapidly, and nothing seems to stop it. Studies of adult addicts and alcoholics show that drug use nearly always starts in the teenage years. Robert L. Dupont, the director of the Center for Behavioral Medicine, says, "New drug use after the age of 20 is almost as uncommon as it was before age 12." Unfortunately, drug use among young people is epidemic. According to the 1982 National Household Survey on Drug Abuse, more than 46 percent of youths aged twelve to seventeen used alcohol in the previous year and more than 20 percent used marijuana. The use of cocaine among youths nearly tripled between 1972 and 1982, from 1.5 percent to 4.3 percent. The use of LSD, stimulants, sedatives, and so-called designer drugs, also has grown. Only heroin use has remained at a constant percentage, although the overall number of heroin users has grown because the population itself continues to grow.

> The author's statement that the statistics are "scary" is an opinion. They are scary to him, but they might not be scary to someone else.

> The author cites a number of statistics to support his view. These are facts.

The most dangerous thing about drug addiction is that it harms many more people than will ever be known. Only the large number of people who die of drug overdoses each year are counted as victims of the drug plague. But many more people die from drug-related problems. These problems include suicide and diseases such as AIDS and hepatitis, which are spread by sharing drug needles. Among people between the ages of fifteen and twenty-four, alcohol-related automobile fatalities are the number one cause of death. The victim of a car crash may not be reported as a "drug" death, but in more than 50 percent of the cases, that is what he or she is.

> The first sentence in this paragraph is an opinion. Other people may hold different opinions about what is most dangerous about drug addiction.

Just as diseases ravage people at home or in a hospital bed, most drug abuse takes place behind closed doors. The casual observer may not realize the extent of the drug problem, but the problem of drug addiction involves more people every day. It is one of the most serious problems we face today.

Is drug addiction a major killer?

The author states that drugs kill more people than is commonly believed. What examples does he give to support this view? Are these facts or opinions?

ADDICTION **11**

VIEWPOINT 2 Addiction is exaggerated

> **Editor's Note:** In this viewpoint, the author maintains that the seriousness of the drug problem has been exaggerated by news organizations. Keep a tally of the facts and opinions the author presents to support his case.

The author's statement that the drug problem is not alarming is an opinion. The author cites statistics to support his views. These statistics are facts.

The author's description of the rise in cocaine use as a "minor change" is an opinion.

The author refers to a study about drug use. The findings of this study are facts.

The author quotes an authority about how the media reports on the drug problem. Is Weisman's statement a fact or an opinion? How can you tell?

Some statements in this paragraph are facts. Which ones? How can you tell?

One statement in this paragraph is a fact. Which statement is it?

According to news reports, drug addiction threatens to destroy the United States. *U.S. News and World Report* called drugs "the nation's No. 1 menace." *Newsweek* reported that drug use is an epidemic "as pervasive [widespread] and as dangerous in its way as the plagues of medieval times." Such news reports are alarming, but the problem of drug addiction is not.

Overall, the percentage of people who use drugs has remained more or less constant for several years. It is true that the use of cocaine has increased. According to the National Institute on Drug Abuse (NIDA), the use of cocaine among high school students increased 1 percent—from 16 to 17 percent—in 1985. The media described that small rise as "a trend." This was an exaggeration. It was a minor change, nothing more.

What the media failed to report is that the same study found a decline in the use of marijuana, stimulants, sedatives, barbiturates, hallucinogens, inhalants, cigarettes, and alcohol among high school students. Meanwhile, the percentage of young people using LSD, PCP, and heroin has held steady. Drug use is not growing rapidly. Only media hype about drug use is growing.

Why does the media exaggerate America's drug problem? Adam Paul Weisman, a reporter who was assigned to write a story about drugs, describes why reporters and editors are attracted to the drug-use story:

> In a way, it was the perfect cover story: sensational, colorful, gruesome, alarmist, with a veneer [thin covering] of social responsibility. Unfortunately, it just wasn't true.

The news organizations—from newspapers to television news programs—are under pressure from their stockholders to produce profits. To do this, they must print cover stories that sell. Television specials about drugs, such as "48 Hours on Crack Street," sell. That program, produced by the Columbia Broadcasting System (CBS), gained the highest rating in five years of any news documentary. Fifteen million people watched it. Such news reports often distort the facts to make the story more interesting.

The August 11, 1986, issue of *Newsweek* reported that there were five million "regular" cocaine users. The figure *Newsweek* used came from the National Institute on Drug Abuse, which stated that "between three and five million used cocaine during the last month." Some of those people no doubt were first-time cocaine users. Others might

12 JUNIORS

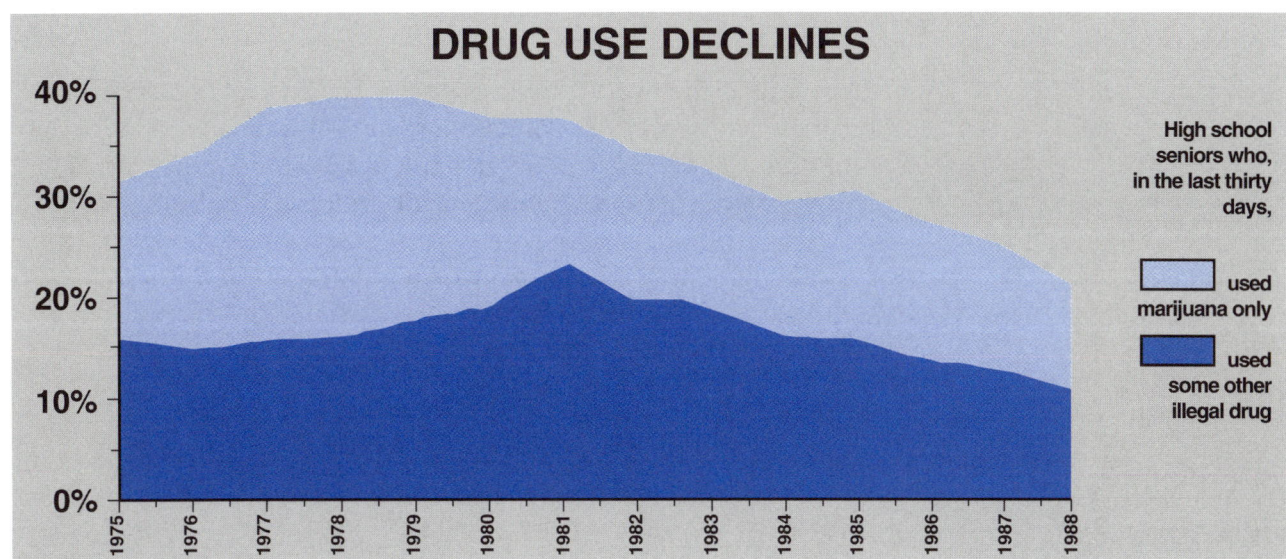

Source: U.S. Department of Health and Human Services

have attended a party that month where cocaine was offered but do not use cocaine every month. In fact, NIDA reports show that only a handful of people—less than 1 percent—use cocaine *or any other illegal drug* on a daily basis. That is bad news for the drug users and their families, but it is not an epidemic. As Abbie Hoffman and Jonathan Silvers put it in their book *Steal This Urine Test*, "Use is not abuse, and habituation is not an addiction. Confusing one for the other leads to distortions and bad conclusions."

The media has painted a bleak picture of drug use in America. A careful review of the facts shows that this picture is distorted. It is the product of media hype.

The author quotes two experts about drug use. Is their statement a fact or an opinion?

Many essays conclude with an opinion. Does this one? How can you tell?

Do profits affect the news?

The author maintains that news organizations distort the news to earn bigger profits. What two examples does the author give to support this view? Are they facts or opinions?

CRITICAL THINKING SKILL 1
Tallying the Facts and Opinions

After reading the two viewpoints on the seriousness of the drug addiction problem, make a chart similar to the ones made for Jan and Ron on page 8. List the facts and opinions each viewpoint gives to make its case. A chart is started for you below.

Viewpoint 1:

FACTS

One out of every ten Americans uses drugs.

OPINIONS

Drug addiction is a crisis of major proportions.

Viewpoint 2:

FACTS

The percentage of people who use drugs has remained constant for several years.

OPINIONS

Media hype about drug use is growing.

Which viewpoint used more factual statements? Which was more convincing? List some facts and opinions that influenced your opinion before you read the viewpoints. Did your opinion change after you read the viewpoints? Why or why not?

CHAPTER 2

PREFACE: Should Addiction Be Treated as a Disease?

According to the American Medical Association (AMA), the nation's largest association of medical doctors, a disease is a disorder that results in the disruption of normal body functions. Since addiction disrupts the normal function of the body and the mind, the AMA has added it to the list of known diseases. Addiction also has specific signs and symptoms, as does any other disease. Doctors point out that while most diseases have one or more known causes, many do not. Addiction, like heart disease, seems to be caused by a number of factors, including heredity, personality, the environment, and poisonous chemicals.

Since the AMA's acceptance of addiction as a disease, thousands of doctors in hospitals and treatment centers across the country have treated drug addicts and alcoholics as medical patients. Most doctors believe that the disease of addiction cannot be cured, but treatment can stop the disease from progressing and can save the patient's life.

The general public and many doctors have had a hard time accepting addiction as a true disease. They believe that taking drugs is a matter of choice. They say that the medical profession has gone along with the disease concept because it means that insurance companies will pay doctors for treatment. These critics point out that most doctors in other countries do not believe that addiction is a disease. Some scientists have even conducted experiments to test the disease concept. Experts differ on the outcome of these experiments.

The following viewpoints debate whether addiction is a disease. Both use facts and opinions to support their arguments. The questions in the margins will help you decide whether some statements are facts or opinions.

VIEWPOINT 3 Addiction should be treated as a disease

Editor's Note: This viewpoint contends that addiction is a disease that overpowers the free will of the addict. Take note of the facts and opinions the author presents.

Drug addiction has been around for centuries. For most of that time, in nearly every part of the world, the problem of drug abuse has been viewed as a moral one; that is, as a choice between good and evil. According to this view, people who take drugs choose to do something bad, just as they might choose to lie, steal, or commit some other evil deed. To stop abusing drugs, according to this belief, the person must reform his or her character. So, ending drug addiction is a matter of willpower, of choosing not to use drugs again.

The author states that the view that drug use is a moral choice is false. Is this a fact or an opinion? Why?

Many people still believe this. For example, in 1988 when then-vice president George Bush was asked how to solve the drug problem, he replied, "By instilling values." This view is comforting to those who hold it, but it is false. Drug addiction is not simply a lifestyle choice. It is a disease. Drug treatment programs that accept addiction as a disease have a chance to succeed. Programs that address addiction as a moral weakness are doomed to fail.

To say addiction is a disease is not just to use an analogy or to make a comparison. It is not to say addiction is *like* a disease, but that it *is* a disease, complete with causes, signs, and symptoms.

Many people have a hard time accepting addiction as a disease.

16 JUNIORS

This is not surprising. Journalist Mary Ellen Pinkham sums up the problem well:

> We tend to think of a disease as something that's caused by a germ (like flu) or that's the result of some system in the body that has gone berserk (as in diabetes or cancer).

Doctors know there is more to disease than that. They note that addiction has three characteristics that define a disease. It is *primary*; that is, it is the source of the problem, not a symptom of another problem. Addiction is also *progressive*: It gets worse over time. As a recovering alcoholic quoted by Kathleen Cahill Tsubata in an article in *The World & I* put it, "Addiction is a fatal illness, if not treated." Addiction is also *chronic*. That means addicts are never cured of the disease. It does not mean addicts cannot be treated for the disease. They can, but they must refrain from using drugs for the rest of their lives. The addict will never reach a point where he or she can tolerate the use of drugs or alcohol.

The American Medical Association, the nation's largest association of medical doctors, has accepted addiction as a disease since 1956. The acceptance of addiction as a disease by doctors is proof that it is a real disease.

The physical nature of addiction makes it a disease. The addict craves drugs to prevent the onset of withdrawal. At the same time, the use of drugs physically impairs the addict's ability to make rational decisions. As William Bennett, the former director of the Office for National Drug Policy, put it, "The addict is a man or woman whose power to exercise . . . rational volition [willpower] . . . has been seriously eroded by drugs, and whose life is instead organized largely—even exclusively—around the pursuit and satisfaction of his addiction." The drug addict is out of control.

Addicts cannot regain control by themselves. They must undergo treatment of some kind. At the very least, they need the support of a group such as Alcoholics Anonymous or Narcotics Anonymous. Some doctors believe additional treatment is needed. Dr. J.K. Phelps, for example, has designed a treatment program that includes the use of vitamins, special foods, and even nonaddicting drugs to help the addict during the withdrawal stage.

New research is revealing all kinds of information about what causes addiction and how it works. These breakthroughs all have their roots in the view that addiction is a disease. These discoveries would not have occurred if scientists had clung to the belief that addiction was a moral and not a scientific question.

The author offers the medical definition of a disease to support his view that addiction is a disease. Is this definition a fact? Why or why not?

Does this paragraph begin with a fact or an opinion? How can you tell?

Do the facts in this paragraph support the author's opinion? Why or why not?

Is the last sentence a fact or an opinion? How do you know?

The body takes charge

When the disease of addiction takes hold, the author states, the body's craving for drugs becomes so strong that the addict cannot simply choose to stop using drugs. What facts does the author present to support this view?

VIEWPOINT 4 Addiction should not be treated as a disease

Editor's Note: In this viewpoint, the author argues that science has not proved that addiction is a disease. In fact, he maintains, research shows that drug use is a matter of personal choice or due to social pressures such as war. Note the facts and opinions the author uses.

The author states that the number of people who question the disease concept of addiction is growing. Is this a fact or an opinion?

"Drug use is a choice, not a disease," wrote psychotherapist Jeffrey A. Schaler in the October/November 1991 issue of *Society* magazine. Schaler is not alone in his belief. A growing number of people are beginning to question the notion that addiction is a disease. Herbert Fingarette, a philosopher at the University of California at Santa Barbara, is one such person. He writes:

> The idea that alcoholism is a disease is a myth, and a harmful myth at at that. The phrase itself—"alcoholism is a disease"—is a slogan. It lacks definite medical meaning and therefore precludes [prevents] one from taking any scientific attitude toward it.

The idea that addiction is a disease was accepted by the American Medical Association almost forty years ago. Because this influential group endorsed the concept of addiction as a disease, many of its members and other scientists began to study addiction in depth. Much of what they found refutes the concept that addiction is a disease.

Are Merry's findings facts or opinions? How can you tell?

For example, in 1966, British psychiatrist Julius Merry found that alcoholics who consumed alcohol, but were unaware of it, did not develop a sudden craving for more alcohol. This finding raised doubts about the belief that small amounts of alcohol trigger a chemical reaction in the "diseased" person's body that makes him or her "lose control."

Which statement in this paragraph is a fact? How does it support the author's opinion about addiction?

The idea that drug use is a choice, not a disease, was bolstered by

GUESS WHICH ONE IS NOT BLAMED FOR THE DRUG PROBLEM?

18 JUNIORS

a study of U.S. soldiers returning from the Vietnam War in 1975. This study, which was paid for by the U.S. Department of Defense, reported on the behavior of 495 soldiers who had tested positive for heroin use when they left Vietnam. After returning to the United States, only 14 percent of these drug users became re-addicted to heroin. Eighty-six percent did not! Considering that heroin is one of the most addictive drugs, this finding was a terrible blow to the idea that addiction is a disease. Lee N. Robins, who led the study, concluded that drug use is the result of external factors such as stress. She and her colleagues wrote:

> It does seem clear that the opiates are not so addictive that use is necessarily followed by addiction nor that once addicted, an individual is necessarily addicted permanently. At least in certain circumstances, individuals can use narcotics regularly and even become addicted to them but yet be able to avoid use in other social circumstances.

The author maintains that the Defense Department study was a "terrible blow" to the belief that addiction is a disease. Is this a fact or an opinion?

So much for the idea that addiction is a "chronic" and "progressive" condition!

The disease model also breaks down when it comes to the matter of drug treatment. Treatment is most effective when the addict decides to kick the habit. If he or she resists treatment, it is less likely to work. Once again, addiction seems to be a matter of choice.

So is the matter of becoming addicted. As Schaler puts it, "A person cannot will the onset of cancer, diabetes or epilepsy. Nor can these diseases be willed away. . . . Drug-taking is not like epilepsy. [It] involves intentional, goal-seeking behavior."

Are Schaler's statements facts or opinions? Is the comparison to epilepsy a good one? Why or why not?

Why do doctors continue to support the concept that addiction is a disease, even when so much evidence exists that it is not? The answer has more to do with money than it does with science. As long as addiction is classified as a disease, insurance companies will pay doctors to treat it.

Some doctors admit that the disease model is false, but they believe it is still useful. This "little white lie" allows addicts to find help for their problem. These doctors forget that this fiction costs non-addicts a billion dollars a year—the amount of money paid out by insurance companies, which collect their money from paying customers.

What fact does the author use here to support his opinion?

The "white lie" approach has another, even more serious flaw. It gives addicts the false impression that they are not responsible for their own lives. It gives them an excuse for their behavior.

A Choice, Not a Disease

The author cites two studies to prove that addiction is a choice, not a disease. Are the results from these studies facts or opinions? Do they prove the author's point? Why or why not?

CRITICAL THINKING SKILL 2
Distinguishing Between Fact and Opinion

This activity will allow you to practice distinguishing between fact and opinion. The statements below are taken from the chapter you have just read about addiction as a disease. Read each statement and consider it carefully. *Mark O for any statement you believe is an opinion, or what someone believes to be true. Mark F for any statement you believe is a fact, or something that can be proved to be true. Mark U for any statement about which you are undecided.*

If you are doing this activity as a member of a class or group, compare your answers with those of other members. You may find that others have different answers than you have. Listening to the reasons others give for their answers can help you learn to distinguish fact from opinion.

EXAMPLE: After returning to the United States from Vietnam, only 14 percent of the American soldiers known to be heroin addicts became re-addicted to heroin.

ANSWER: Fact. This statement could be proved by looking at statistics of heroin use among Vietnam veterans.

Answer

1. Drug use is a choice, not a disease. _____

2. The American Medical Association has accepted addiction as a disease since 1956. _____

3. Drug treatment programs that accept addiction as a disease have a chance to succeed. _____

4. Only 14 percent of Vietnam veterans became re-addicted to heroin. _____

5. Addicts cannot regain control by themselves. _____

6. The idea that alcoholism is a disease is a myth, and a harmful myth at that. _____

7. Addiction is not simply a lifestyle choice. It is a a disease. _____

CHAPTER 3

PREFACE: Should Drugs Be Legalized?

A hundred years ago, several drugs that are now illegal were sold openly in the United States. The beverage Coca-Cola contained small amounts of cocaine, which is made from the leaves of the coca plant. Laudanum, a common sleeping aid, was made from opium. These drugs were also used in higher dosages by large numbers of people, often at the recommendation of their doctors.

As knowledge about drug addiction grew, many people became concerned about drug use. In response to these concerns, Congress passed the Pure Food and Drug Act in 1906. Under this law, the makers of products that contained opium and other drugs had to label their products so the public would know that the products contained addictive chemicals. In 1914, the government went even further. Congress passed the Harrison Narcotics Act barring the sale of opium and coca. At first, doctors could continue to give these drugs to patients who were addicted to them, but later even these uses were banned.

As soon as these drugs were banned, smugglers started to sneak the illegal substances into the country and sell them to addicts and casual users. An article that appeared in the *Illinois Medical Journal* in 1926 described the new trade in illegal drugs: "Instead of stopping the traffic, those who deal in dope now make double their money from the poor unfortunates upon whom they prey." In the 1920s the government banned heroin, and in the 1930s it banned marijuana. With these actions, the illegal drug trade grew even larger.

Today, Americans spend $150 billion on illegal drugs, according to the members of a congressional task force that studied the illegal drug trade in the United States. Drug trafficking is big business, and it has spawned a host of social problems. Drug lords often fight to control their markets, leading to drug-related violence. Drug addicts often turn to prostitution or theft to pay the high cost of illegal drugs. According to government statistics, 50 percent of the inmates in federal prisons committed some sort of drug-related crime.

In the following chapter, viewpoint 5 contends that if the drug laws were repealed, the trade in illegal drugs would collapse and many social problems would be instantly solved. Viewpoint 6 argues that drug laws serve the useful purpose of preventing addiction and should be fully enforced. As you read these viewpoints, take note of their use of facts and opinions.

VIEWPOINT 5 Legalizing drugs would reduce addiction

> **Editor's Note:** This viewpoint argues that drug laws are the real cause of most of the problems people associate with drug use. Does the author use facts or opinions to support his views?

The author describes a scene in a park. Is this story a fact or an opinion? Explain.

Do you agree with the author's opinion about the drug addict? Why or why not?

Is the first statement in this paragraph a fact or an opinion? Why?

The author provides a statistic for drug-related murders. Is this statistic a fact or an opinion? How does it support the author's point?

A cocaine addict approaches two teenage boys in a park and starts talking to them. Pretty soon the conversation gets around to what the boys do for fun. The addict describes the great feeling he gets from using cocaine. He even offers to share his cocaine with the boys. Of course, this addict is not looking for new friends. He is looking for new customers. He is a drug pusher. He sells drugs so he can pay for his own drug habit. He wants the boys to try cocaine. He hopes they will enjoy using it and want to start buying it.

Most people watching this scene would say that the addict is an awful person, willing to recruit young people to feed his habit. These people would be wrong. The real reason that the addict does this is because he is forced to: The laws we have against buying, selling, or taking drugs are at fault. By enforcing these laws, the police make drugs like cocaine hard to get. Because the drugs are hard to get, they cost a lot of money—much more money than it costs to make them. Since the addict does not earn enough money at his job to pay for his drug habit, he turns to selling drugs to make the extra money he needs.

If drugs like cocaine were legal, they would cost much less. The addict could afford to buy them without needing to sell drugs or recruit new users. "If you take the profit out of drug trafficking," argues Kurt Schmoke, the mayor of Baltimore, "you won't have children hiding drugs [for pushers] for $100 a night or wearing beepers to school because it makes more sense to run drugs for someone than to take some of the jobs that are available." By reducing the cost of drugs, legalization would reduce the number of drug pushers, the number of drug users, and the number of addicts.

Repealing the drug laws would solve many other problems usually blamed on drugs. For example, it would reduce the number of drug-related murders. In 1987, 130 drug-related murders were committed in Washington, D.C., alone. Most drug-related murders are the result of "turf wars." These wars are fought by drug pushers who are often members of gangs. They fight to keep other pushers off their turf; that is, out of their area. Drugs are not the cause of these wars. Drug laws are. The laws force drug prices so high that it makes sense to some people to fight for the opportunity to sell the illegal substances.

Legalized drugs could be taxed just as cigarettes and alcohol are, raising billions of dollars for the government. This money could be used to fund drug treatment centers. The government would also save money that is now spent on enforcing drug laws. Federal, state, and

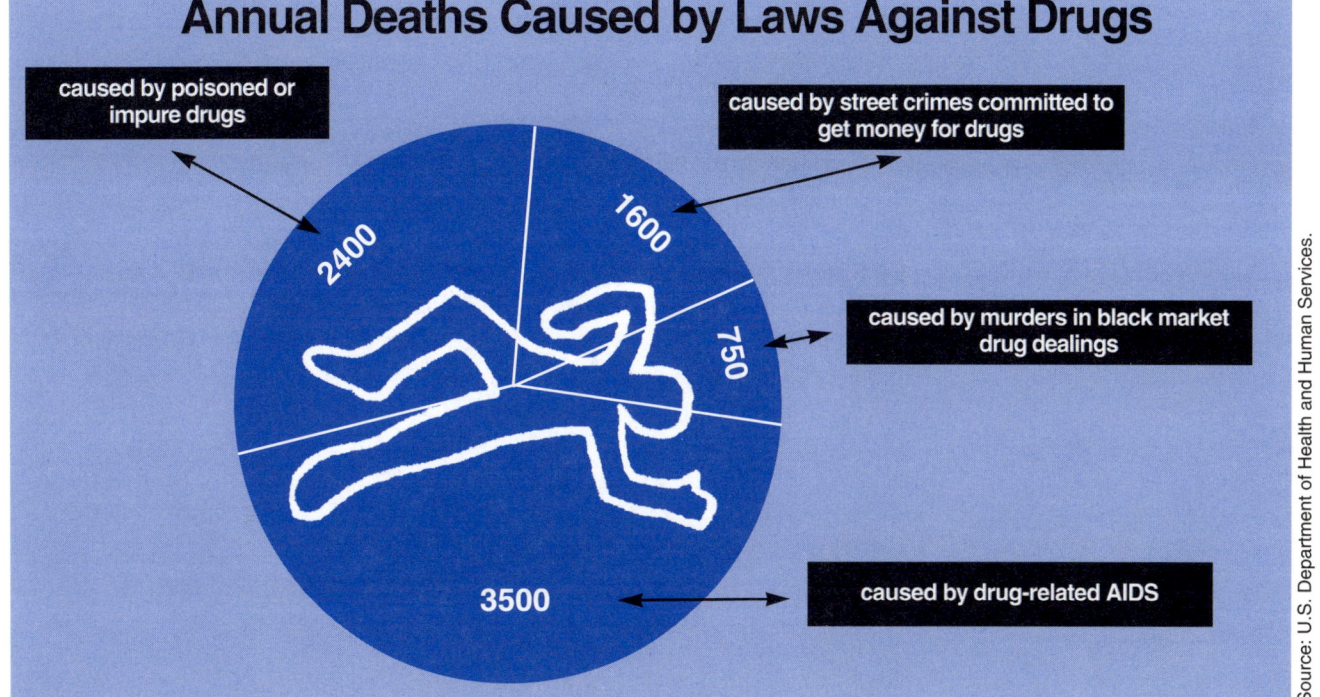

local governments spend more than $8 billion a year on direct drug law enforcement, according to Ethan A. Nadelmann, a law professor at the Woodrow Wilson School of Public and International Affairs at Princeton University.

"The fight against drugs for the past 70 years has been one long glorious failure," says Joseph McNamara, the chief of police in San Jose, California. "The courts are overflowing, there is violence on the streets, and the problem seems to be getting worse," he states. McNamara is right. The "war on drugs" has not reduced the amount of drugs available, the number of users, the number of addicts, or the number of crimes committed to obtain drugs. It is time to try a new approach.

Legalizing drugs would reduce crime by taking the profit out of the illegal drug market. It would reduce drug addiction by decreasing the number of pushers who try to recruit new users. And it would raise money so the government could provide more drug treatment and drug education programs. Now is the time to make drugs legal.

Is the cost the author gives for drug enforcement fact or opinion?

The author quotes a law enforcement expert about the drug war. Is the expert's statement a fact or an opinion?

How does this article conclude, with facts or opinions? How can you tell?

Are drug laws to blame?

The author argues that drug laws do more harm than good. Name two bad effects of drug laws, according to the author. Are these effects facts or opinions?

VIEWPOINT 6 Legalizing drugs would increase addiction

Editor's Note: Legalizing drugs like cocaine and marijuana would be a disaster, according to this viewpoint. What facts does the author present to persuade you of the dangers of legalization?

Does this paragraph express facts or opinions? How can you tell?

Does the author support his conclusion that more crime would result from legalization with facts? How can you tell?

The author cites estimates about drug use. Are these figures facts or opinions?

A dangerous idea is getting a lot of serious attention these days. It is the idea that legalizing drugs would solve many of the problems we face today. This idea is nonsense. Legalizing dangerous drugs would only make things worse.

The first claim made by those who want to legalize drugs is that crime would be reduced. No doubt the number of some crimes would be reduced. The buying, selling, and use of drugs would no longer be crimes, so those crimes would go down. On the other hand, certain crimes would go up. Some drugs, such as PCP, cause violent behavior. The number of crimes committed by people using these drugs would increase.

The crime of driving under the influence of drugs or alcohol would also increase. Right now the total number of drug users is about 23 million people. That number would likely increase to between 50 and 100 million, according to Morton K. Kondracke, an editor for the *New Republic*. Kondracke writes that during Prohibition, when alcohol was illegal, alcohol usage was "a third or a fourth of its former level." Using

24 JUNIORS

these figures as a guide, Kondracke states, "It seems fair to estimate that use of drugs will at least double, and possibly triple, if the price is cut, supplies are readily available, and society's sanction is lifted." That means that the number of drivers under the influence of drugs—and the traffic deaths they cause—will also double or triple. Alcohol-related traffic accidents are the leading cause of death among people between the ages of fifteen and twenty-four. The legalization of drugs would only add to that already monstrous statistic.

Supporters of legalization say that a lower price for drugs would take away the need for addicts to steal. They assume that drug addicts would be able to afford low-cost drugs. But hard-core addicts are unable to hold jobs or earn money in an honest way. Even if a dose of heroin costs only five dollars, the addict would have to steal the five dollars to get it.

Supporters of legalization also suggest that taking the profit out of drugs will destroy the gangs that control the drug trade in many cities. But "there would always be opportunities for those who saw profit in peddling larger quantities, or improved versions, of products that are forbidden or restricted," wrote Charles B. Rangel, the chairman of the House Select Committee on Narcotics Abuse and Control. Because the government would heavily tax drugs, the legal price would remain above the street price, creating an opening for a black market to form.

One of the major benefits of drug legalization, according to its proponents, is that the government would be able to use the drug taxes to pay for drug treatment programs and education. But there would not be a tax windfall from low-cost drugs. As Kondracke points out, "Total taxes collected right now from alcohol sales at the local, state, and federal levels come to only $13.1 billion per year—which is a pittance compared to the damage done to society as a result of alcohol abuse." The story would be the same with legalized drugs. The small amount of money raised by taxes would never pay for the high cost of educating students or treating the many people who would become addicted to the legalized drugs. Millions of adults who otherwise would never even get close to the stuff would experiment with drugs. Many would get hooked. Drug addiction, already a major public health problem, would become a crisis.

Does the author's use of statistical facts support his viewpoint? If so, how? If not, why not?

Is the author's prediction about a black market a fact or an opinion? How can you tell?

Is Kondracke's conclusion based on fact or opinion?

Faulty logic?

The author states that legalization would not solve the problems that its proponents say it would. Name two things the author says would not be solved by legalization. Are these facts or opinions?

CRITICAL THINKING SKILL 3
Understanding Editorial Cartoons

Throughout this book, cartoons illustrate the ideas in the viewpoints. Editorial cartoons are an effective and usually humorous way of presenting an opinion on an issue. While many cartoons are easy to understand, some, like the one below, require more thought.

This cartoon deals with the subject of drug legalization. The man who is speaking is comparing legal drugs—alcohol and tobacco—with illegal drugs. What do the charts he is using suggest about the consumption rates of legal drugs compared to illegal drugs? What does he think would happen to the consumption rate of tobacco and alcohol if they were made illegal? What do you think this suggests about the consumption rate of illegal drugs? Does the cartoonist think that the consumption rate of illegal drugs would go up or down if they were legalized? How can you tell? Do you think he favors legalization? Why?

Do the charts in the cartoon represent facts or opinions? Are the speaker's words facts or opinions? Explain your answers.

If you are doing this exercise with a class or group, discuss your answers with other members of the class or group. Do they agree or disagree with you?

Asay, by permission of the *Colorado Springs Gazette Telegraph*.

CHAPTER

PREFACE: **What Should the Government Do to Reduce Addiction?**

Most politicians believe the government should do more to reduce addiction, but they disagree about how to do it.

Some people, like former president Richard Nixon and former director of the Office of National Drug Control Policy, William J. Bennett, believe the solution to the drug problem lies in tougher enforcement of drug laws. "We need a total war against drugs," wrote Nixon, who declared the first "war on drugs" in 1971. In 1972, Congress responded to Nixon's call for action by spending $1 billion on drug law enforcement. The next year, Nixon declared, "We have turned the corner on drug addiction in America." Even though little evidence existed to support this claim, Congress reduced funding in the fight against drugs.

The federal government did little about drugs until the 1980s, when Presidents Reagan and Bush spent more than $16 billion to fight a second drug "war." President Bush made William Bennett his "drug czar." Bennett's job was to coordinate the government's campaign against drugs. Based on figures that showed a decline in the use of cocaine and marijuana, Bennett announced that the war against drugs was succeeding. Jeffrey A. Eisenach, a researcher at the Heritage Foundation, agreed: "If lawmakers continue to improve on current policies, . . . the drug problem can be overcome."

Other experts disagree. They say that the government's war against drug suppliers and users is a failure. They point out that although the government reported a 4,000 percent increase in cocaine seizures in the 1980s, the street price of cocaine actually declined by as much as 50 percent. U.S. Customs officials admit that they seize only 10 percent of the drugs entering the United States. These experts believe the government should focus more of its efforts on reducing the demand for drugs. They suggest that the government spend more money for the treatment of drug addicts and for drug education.

The following viewpoints debate what the government should do to reduce drug addiction. Pay attention to how each uses facts and opinions in its arguments.

VIEWPOINT 7 The government should spend more on drug law enforcement

Editor's Note: Better enforcement of drug laws will reduce addiction, according to this viewpoint. Without this step, any other programs to reduce addiction will fail, it argues. Watch for the use of facts and opinions as the viewpoint's argument takes shape.

What does the author say needs to be done to solve the drug problem? Is this a fact or an opinion? How can you tell?

The author quotes Bennett to add credibility to his own opinion that more law enforcement is needed. How would Bennett's position as a government official affect his opinion?

Does the author use facts or opinions in this paragraph?

What effect does drug use have on poverty, according to the author? Is this a fact or an opinion? How can you tell?

Enforcing drug laws costs taxpayers billions of dollars. This does not mean that we should give up the war on drugs, however. On the contrary, the only way to solve the drug problem is to spend more money on law enforcement. As former president Nixon put it, "We need a total war against drugs. Total war means war on all fronts against an enemy with many faces."

The first responsibility of government is to protect its citizens. Right now, however, our government is not doing that very well. In many of our largest cities, whole neighborhoods are under siege because of drug-related crime. Addicts who cannot pay their debts are murdered. Drugs are sold in open-air markets near schools. Drug paraphernalia litters the streets. These conditions must be changed before drug addiction can be reduced. As William Bennett, the former director of the Office of National Drug Control Policy, put it:

> The rehabilitation of a community cannot begin until some degree of fundamental order and basic civility has been established. Treatment and education stand little chance of succeeding if they must compete in a neighborhood where drugs and drug dealers flourish on every corner.

We can tell kids not to use drugs, but as long as they see users and pushers on a daily basis, drugs will still have some attraction. We can tell our young people to not get involved in gangs and the drug business, but as long as the richest person in the neighborhood is a drug dealer, no one is going to listen. We must get drugs off the streets before we can hope to get them off the minds and out of the hands of potential users. This is one case where something needs to be out of sight before it is truly out of mind.

Some people say that the government should spend its money eliminating the causes of drug use, rather than enforcing the laws against it. Certainly there are factors that seem to promote drug use. Areas with high unemployment, poor schools, and widespread poverty tend to have higher levels of drug use than do communities in which more people have jobs and money. But even within poorer communities, the vast majority of people are able to resist drugs, so poverty cannot be said to *cause* drug use. At most, poverty weakens the "immune system" of the community, as William Bennett puts it. "Drugs are the invading virus. And you must attack the virus while you are pondering how to strengthen the immune system," he declares.

28 JUNIORS

Asay, by permission of the *Colorado Springs Gazette Telegraph*.

In fact, no efforts to reduce poverty will succeed without attacking the drug problem first. "Drugs have destroyed more families than poverty ever did," says John Jacob, the president of the Urban League. Drugs have the power to break up families, decrease work productivity, and disrupt schooling—all the things that are needed to create wealth.

This is why most of the cries for help in the war against drugs come from the communities hardest hit by the effects of drugs. Across the country, citizens have banded together to force drugs out of their communities. Residents on Thomas Avenue in Saint Paul, Minnesota, marched in front of a crack house until they got it moved off their street. In Oakland, Houston, and New York, neighborhoods have formed walking patrols to harass pushers peddling their deadly wares. The people in the communities most hurt by drugs are asking for more law enforcement, not less. That is the least they deserve.

Do these factual examples enhance the author's point about law enforcement? Why or why not?

Cause or effect?

The author maintains that poverty does not cause drug use. Do you agree or disagree? What examples does the author give to prove his theory that drug use causes poverty?

VIEWPOINT 8 The government should spend more on drug treatment

Editor's Note: Drug addiction will never be reduced unless the government addresses its root causes, argues this viewpoint. Remember to watch for facts and opinions as you read.

The author offers no factual support for his opinions. Nevertheless, do you find his argument convincing? Why or why not?

The government's war on drugs is failing. Law enforcement officials and politicians call for more money to carry on this war, but more dollars spent on law enforcement will not make a difference. That is because law enforcement focuses on the effects of drug use rather than on its causes. As long as the demand for drugs exists, someone will be there to supply them. To cut down on demand, the government must address its causes.

What causes drug use? A lack of education about drugs, for one thing. Many schools have drug awareness programs, but these are often the first victims of budget cuts. Volunteers try to make up for this loss, but their efforts are simply not enough to counteract the constant pressure on young people to use drugs.

How many facts does the author use in this paragraph? Do they make his point about drug use more convincing? Why or why not?

Poverty also causes drug use. Among black men, for example, unemployment is two to three times higher than the national average. Many who do have jobs do not earn as much as they used to. Real wages dropped by 50 percent for black men during the 1970s. Such conditions cause feelings of despair and hopelessness. Drugs offer a sure, if temporary, escape from these feelings. Not surprisingly then, drug addiction is rampant in poor communities. To reduce drug addiction, the government should do more to provide jobs and decent

30 JUNIORS

wages to our poorest people. Instead, government spends more on police operations to try to arrest users and suppliers. Politicians miss the point—give these people jobs and they will not need drugs to numb their pain and disappointment.

Another way to reduce addiction is to increase treatment programs for those who are dependent on drugs. Right now, thousands of people are on waiting lists to join drug treatment programs. No one who wants to stop using drugs should have to wait for help. Unfortunately, there are not enough government-sponsored treatment programs. An addict can be treated in a month-long program for between $6,000 and $12,000 dollars. Sound expensive? Not when you consider that it costs $71,600 in salary and benefits to put a single police officer on the streets for a year. As the *Los Angeles Times* put it in a 1990 editorial, "Police can help stop drug abuse, but treatment costs less and does more good."

Treatment is also a real bargain when compared to the cost of caring for babies born to drug addicts. The cost of caring for one such child after birth far exceeds the cost of putting his or her mother through treatment prior to birth. According to a 1988 study by the National Association for Perinatal Addiction Research and Education (NAPARE), 10 percent of new mothers used drugs during pregnancy. Seventy-five percent of those new mothers used cocaine. Not all of their babies were born addicted, but many of those who were not addicted suffered from other physical problems. "In Washington, D.C., the infant mortality rate, already among the highest in the U.S., increased by nearly 50 percent in the first half of 1989 because of a surge of babies born to cocaine-addicted women," reported the *Lincoln Review*. Women who are pregnant should be able to enroll in drug treatment programs upon demand, but no money is available. It is being spent on law enforcement.

The public feels safer when their politicians decry the drug problem and say we need more laws, more police, and bigger prisons. But this will do little to steer drug addicts from their impoverished lives. Government must work to prevent addiction by offering real alternatives—jobs, treatment, and a chance for a meaningful life.

What facts does the author use to prove his point about treatment being cost effective? Do you find his point convincing? Why or why not?

How does the author use statistical facts to support his opinions in this paragraph?

The roots of the problem

The author maintains that our current drug policy does not address the causes of drug addiction. What facts does he provide to support this belief?

CRITICAL THINKING SKILL 4: Using Facts and Opinions

Write two paragraphs on one of the topics listed below. Make sure to use facts in the first paragraph and opinions in the second. Two sample paragraphs are provided to help you.

Topics
Poverty causes drug abuse.
Drug abuse causes poverty.
Drug treatment costs less than drug law enforcement.
The war on drugs is succeeding.
The war on drugs is failing.

SAMPLE 1 (Facts)

Social pressure causes addiction.

    Drugs alone do not cause addiction, according to a United States government study of Vietnam veterans. In the study, Vietnam veterans who had used heroin during the war were monitored once they returned home. Only 14 percent of the soldiers continued to use heroin once they had been removed from the war zone. This finding suggests that the stress of war caused the soldiers to turn to drugs. Once the stress was removed, the addiction ceased. Drug addiction is not a primary disease, as some people say. It is a symptom of other problems.

SAMPLE 2 (Opinions)

Profits cause the media to distort the drug story.

    Each day, the editors of newspapers and the producers of TV and radio news programs must decide which news stories to cover. They will tell you that they base their decisions on the public's "right to know," but this is a sham. The news is big business, and these decision makers choose their stories based on profits, not ideals. They know that bad news outsells good news and that disasters sell best of all. That is why the media portray the drug problem as a "plague" or an "epidemic" or a "war." The media do not care whether the story is true, only that it sells.

FOR FURTHER READING

The author recommends the following books and periodicals for further research on the topic. Check Works Consulted for further suggestions.

American Medical Association, "Drug Abuse in the United States," *Journal of the American Medical Association*, April 24, 1991.

Dan Baum, "The War on Drugs, Twelve Years Later," *ABA Journal*, March 1993. Available from the American Bar Association, 750 N. Lake Shore Dr., Chicago, IL 60611.

Elliott Currie, *Reckoning: Drugs, the Cities, and the American Future*. New York: Hill & Wang, 1993.

Vince Fox, *Addiction, Change, and Choice: The New View of Alcoholism*. Tucson: See Sharp Press, 1993.

Marc Galanter, "The End of Addiction," *Psychology Today*, November/December 1992.

Dean R. Gerstein and Lawrence W. Green, eds., *Preventing Drug Abuse*. Washington, DC: National Academy Press, 1993.

Gerald W. Lynch and Roberta Blotner, "Legalizing Drugs Is Not the Solution," *America*, February 13, 1993.

Richard Lawrence Miller, *The Case for Legalizing Drugs*. New York: Praeger, 1991.

Stanton Peele and Archie Brodsky, *The Truth About Addiction and Recovery*. New York: Simon & Schuster, 1992.

Barry Stimmel, *The Facts About Drug Use*. Binghamton, NY: Haworth Press, 1992.

Joseph B. Treaster, "Some Think the 'War on Drugs' Is Being Waged on the Wrong Front," *The New York Times*, July 28, 1992.

WORKS CONSULTED

The following books and periodicals were used in the compilation of this book.

William F. Alden, "The Scope of the Drug Problem," *Vital Speeches of the Day*, October 1, 1986. Provides statistics on drug usage in the United States.

William J. Bennett, "Responding to New Challenges in the War on Drugs." A speech delivered at the Heritage Foundation, March 20-21, 1990. Argues that law enforcement efforts should be increased as a first step toward controlling drug use.

George J. Church, "Thinking the Unthinkable," *Time*, May 30, 1988. Describes the growing movement to legalize drugs.

Alfonse D'Amato, "The Drug War Can Be Won," *USA Today*, July 1990. Maintains that the war on drugs can be won if an international antinarcotics strike force is created.

Robert L. DuPont Jr., *Getting Tough on Gateway Drugs*. Washington, DC: American Psychiatric Press, 1984. Describes causes and cures for the drug epidemic.

Herbert Fingarette, "Alcoholism: The Mythical Disease," *The Public Interest*, Spring 1988. Argues that alcoholism is not a disease.

Ronald Hamowy, *Dealing with Drugs*. Lexington, MA: D.C. Heath, 1987. Contains an essay by Randy E. Barnett, associate law professor at the Chicago-Kent College of Law, who argues in support of legalizing drugs.

Morton M. Kondracke, "Don't Legalize Drugs," *The New Republic*, June 27, 1988. Challenges the arguments in favor of legalizing drugs.

The Lincoln Review, "The Scourge of Drug Addiction: A Challenge for the Black Community," Winter 1990. Describes drug usage among blacks and how community action can win the war on drugs.

Los Angeles Times, "Rehabilitation: Way to Conquer Crack," May 20, 1990. Argues that drug treatment costs less and does more good than increased law enforcement.

Ethan A. Nadelmann, "The Case for Legalization," *The Public Interest*, Summer 1988. Describes the benefits of legalizing some drugs.

Richard Nixon, *In the Arena: A Memoir of Victory, Defeat, and Renewal*. New York: Simon and Schuster, 1990. Maintains that zero tolerance is the only way to reduce illegal drug use.

Mary Ellen Pinkham, *How to Stop the One You Love from Drinking*. New York: Putnam, 1986. Discusses the author's struggle with alcoholism and explains why addiction is considered a disease.

Charles B. Rangel, "Legalize Drugs? Not on Your Life," *The New York Times*, May 17, 1988. Describes the pitfalls of legalizing drugs.

Kathryn Schierl, "A Proposal to Illinois Legislatures: Revise the Illinois Criminal Code to Include Criminal Sanctions Against Prenatal Substance Abusers," *The John Marshall Law Review*, vol. 23, pg. 393, 1990.

Eric A. Voth, "Addiction as a Primary Disease," *Drug Awareness Information Newsletter*, September 1987. Provides a medical definition for the disease of alcoholism.

Adam Paul Weisman, "I Was a Drug-Hype Junkie," *The New Republic*, October 6, 1986. Describes the pressure on writers to make drug abuse seem like an ever-increasing problem.

Jann S. Wenner, "Drug War: A New Vietnam?" *The New York Times*, June 23, 1990. Argues that the war on drugs creates more problems than it solves.

Dennis Wholey, *The Courage to Change*. New York: Houghton Mifflin, 1984. Includes an interview with G. Douglas Talbott, M.D., director of the Ridgeview Institute for Alcohol and Drug Problems in Smyrna, Georgia, who says that alcoholism is the most treatable untreated disease in the country.

Stephen Wisotsky, *Beyond the War on Drugs*. Buffalo: Prometheus Books, 1990. Maintains that because the war on drugs has failed, federal drug policies should be reevaluated.

Robert Wright, "Alcohol and Free Will," *The New Republic*, December 14, 1987. Argues that the disease-concept of alcoholism does not withstand scientific or philosophical scrutiny.

ORGANIZATIONS TO CONTACT

The following organizations are concerned with the issues debated in this book. All of them have publications or information available for interested readers.

American Civil Liberties Union (ACLU)
132 W. 43rd St.
New York, NY 10036
(212) 944-9800

The ACLU, one of the oldest civil liberties organizations in the United States, favors the decriminalization of drugs. The ACLU publishes information packets on drug legalization, decriminalization, and public smoking.

American Society of Addiction Medicine (ASAM)
5225 Wisconsin Ave. NW, Suite 409
Washington, DC 20015
(202) 244-8948

The society is a group of physicians with special interest and experience in the field of alcoholism and other drug dependencies. It believes all addicts should have access to government-funded drug and alcohol treatment. The society publishes the quarterly *Journal of Addictive Diseases*, the bimonthly *ASAM News* newsletter, and public policy statements on alcoholism and drug dependency.

Center for Alcohol Studies
Rutgers University
Smithers Hall, Busch Campus
Piscataway, NJ 08854
(201) 932-2190

The center contains a large library on alcohol-related topics and provides information on the use and abuse of alcohol. It publishes the quarterly *Journal of Studies on Alcohol* as well as bibliographies on the psychological, social, and physiological aspects of alcoholism.

Do It Now Foundation
6423 S. Ash Ave.
Tempe, AZ 85283
(602) 257-0797

The foundation fights drug abuse by providing students and adults with facts on legal and illegal drugs and drug abuse. Founded in 1968, Do It Now offered one of the first drug-abuse hotline services in the country. The foundation publishes books, posters, and taped public-service announcements on drug abuse as well as the pamphlets *Guide for Young People, Total Recovery,* and *Everyday Detox: A Guide to Living Without Chemicals.*

Drug and Crime Data Center and Clearinghouse
1600 Research Blvd.
Rockville, MD 20850
(800) 666-3332

The clearinghouse, an office of the U.S. Justice Department, compiles and distributes information on drug-related crime for use by policymakers and researchers. Its publications include *Federal Drug Data for National Policy* and *State Drug Resources: A National Directory*.

Drug Policy Foundation
4801 Massachusetts Ave. NW, #400
Washington, DC 20016-2087
(202) 895-1634

The foundation supports legalizing many drugs. It believes that increasing the number of treatment programs for addicts can reduce the demand for drugs. Its publications include the bimonthly *Drug Policy Letter* and the books *The Great Drug War* and *1989-1990, A Reformer's Catalogue*. It also distributes *Press Clips*, an annual compilation of newspaper articles on drug legalization issues.

INDEX

addiction
  as a disease, 6, 15, 16-17
    con, 18-19
    causes for classification
      doctors' greed, 19
  as exaggerated, 12-13
  as self-induced, 7
  as serious problem, 10-11
  causes of
    high cost of drugs, 22
  solutions to
    legalization of drugs, 22-23
      con, 24-25
    need for government
      involvement, 27
    need for more treatment, 30-31
  symptoms of, 17
AIDS, 11
Alcoholics Anonymous, 17
alcoholism
  as a disease, 17
  myth of, 18
Alden, William F., 10-11
American Medical Association
  criticism of, 18
  definition of disease, 15
  position on addiction as a
    disease, 6, 17
automobile fatalities
  number of addicts who die in, 11

Bennett, William J., 17, 27, 28
Bush, George, 16, 27

Coca-Cola, 21
cocaine
  legalization of
    as positive, 22
  number of teens who use, 11
    as increasing, 12
    con, 13
Coleman, Vernon, 10

disease
  definition of, 17
doctors
  greed and addiction, 19
drug-addicted babies
  cost of caring for, 19
drug law enforcement
  more reliance on will reduce
    drug use, 27
    con, 30
  need to increase, 28
drug laws
  need to repeal, 22-23
drugs

cost of
  as cause of addiction, 22
  con, 25
destruction of families and, 29
illegal use of, 9
legalization of, 21
  as increasing addiction, 24-25
  con, 22-23
  would make taxable, 22
number of Americans who use,
  10-11
  as not increasing, 12-13
widespread sale of, 28
drug use
  as not increasing, 12-13
drunk driving
  would increase if drugs were
    legalized, 24-25
Dupont, Robert L., 11

education
  need for, 30
Eisenach, Jeffrey A., 27

Federal Bureau of Investigation
  statistics on drug use, 9
Fingarette, Herbert, 18

gangs
  as caused by drug-dealing, 22
  would not be destroyed by
    drug legalization, 25
government
  addiction and
    should do more to reduce,
      28-29
    should fund more treatment,
      30-31

Harrison Narcotics Act, 21
Hoffman, Abbie, 13

Jacob, John, 29

Kondracke, Morton K., 24

McNamara, Joseph 23
media
  as exaggerating the drug
    problem, 12-13
Merry, Julius, 18

Nadelmann, Ethan A., 23
Narcotics Anonymous, 17
National Association for
  Perinatal Addiction Research
  and Education, 31

National Household Survey on
  Drug Abuse, 11
National Institute on Drug Abuse,
  12
Nixon, Richard, 27, 28

opium, 21

Phelps, J.K., 17
Pinkham, Mary Ellen, 16-17
poverty
  as cause of drug abuse, 30-31
  con, 28
pregnancy
  should be criteria for access to
    treatment, 31
prohibition
  drawbacks to, 24-25
Pure Food and Drug Act, 21

Rangel, Charles B., 25
Reagan, Ronald, 27
Robins, Lee N., 19

Schaler, Jeffrey A., 18, 19
Schmoke, Kurt, 22
suicide
  number of addicts who commit,
    11

taxes
  from legal drug sales, 22
  on legalized drugs
    would increase cost, 25
teenagers
  number who become addicted,
    11
  number involved in drug
    dealing, 22
  use of cocaine increasing
    among, 12
The National Institute on
  Alcohol Abuse, 11
treatment programs
  as unsuccessful, 7
  need for, 16, 17, 27, 30-31
  success of dependent on
    addicts' will power, 19
Tsubata, Kathleen Cahill, 17

Vietnam War veterans
  drug studies with, 19

war on drugs, 27
  as failing, 30-31
  need for, 28-29
Weisman, Adam Paul, 12